50 Legendary Ocean Recipes

By: Kelly Johnson

Table of Contents

- Lobster Newberg
- Grilled Swordfish
- Seared Tuna with Sesame Seeds
- Clam Chowder
- Shrimp Scampi
- Paella
- Baked Salmon with Dill
- Fish Tacos
- Lobster Bisque
- Oysters Rockefeller
- Tuna Tartare
- Mussels in White Wine Sauce
- Crab Cakes
- Fish and Chips
- Shrimp Cocktail
- Crab Legs with Garlic Butter
- Grilled Mahi Mahi
- Smoked Salmon
- Shrimp and Grits
- Seafood Risotto
- Lobster Roll
- Grilled Octopus
- Shrimp Alfredo
- Clams Casino
- Salmon with Mango Salsa
- Ceviche
- Scallops with Lemon Butter
- Crab Stuffed Mushrooms
- Blackened Snapper
- Tuna Poke Bowl
- Baked Cod with Herb Crust
- Grilled Shrimp Skewers
- Fish Stew
- Lobster Mac and Cheese
- Shrimp Tempura

- Scallops and Asparagus
- Mussels Marinara
- Crab Louie Salad
- Lobster Tail with Garlic Butter
- Fried Catfish
- Crab and Corn Chowder
- Mahi Mahi with Pineapple Salsa
- Shrimp and Lobster Ravioli
- Smoked Fish Dip
- Fish Casserole
- Clam Bake
- Grilled Tuna Steaks
- Salmon Croquettes
- Fish En Papillote
- Shrimp and Spinach Salad

Lobster Newberg

Ingredients:

- 2 lobster tails, cooked and chopped
- 4 large eggs
- 1/2 cup heavy cream
- 1/4 cup brandy (such as Cognac)
- 1 tablespoon butter
- 1 tablespoon Dijon mustard
- 1/2 teaspoon paprika
- Salt and pepper to taste
- 1/4 cup fresh parsley, chopped
- Toasted bread or pastry shells for serving

Instructions:

1. **Prepare the lobster:**
   Remove the lobster meat from the tails and chop it into bite-sized pieces. Set aside.
2. **Make the sauce:**
   In a double boiler, whisk together eggs and heavy cream until smooth. Slowly add the brandy and cook, whisking constantly, until the mixture thickens. Remove from heat and stir in butter, mustard, paprika, salt, and pepper.
3. **Combine lobster and sauce:**
   Add the chopped lobster to the egg mixture and stir gently. Return to heat for a minute to warm through.
4. **Serve:**
   Spoon the lobster Newberg onto toasted bread or in pastry shells and garnish with chopped parsley. Serve immediately.

Grilled Swordfish

Ingredients:

- 2 swordfish steaks (about 1-inch thick)
- 2 tablespoons olive oil
- 1 teaspoon lemon zest
- 2 tablespoons lemon juice
- 1 teaspoon garlic powder
- 1 teaspoon dried oregano
- Salt and pepper to taste

Instructions:

1. **Prepare the marinade:**
   In a small bowl, combine olive oil, lemon zest, lemon juice, garlic powder, oregano, salt, and pepper.
2. **Marinate the swordfish:**
   Coat the swordfish steaks in the marinade and let them sit for 15-20 minutes.
3. **Grill the swordfish:**
   Preheat your grill to medium-high heat. Grill the swordfish for 4-5 minutes per side, or until the fish is cooked through and has grill marks.
4. **Serve:**
   Serve the grilled swordfish with additional lemon wedges and a side of vegetables or salad.

Seared Tuna with Sesame Seeds

Ingredients:

- 2 tuna steaks (about 6 oz each)
- 2 tablespoons sesame oil
- 2 tablespoons black sesame seeds
- 2 tablespoons white sesame seeds
- Salt and pepper to taste
- Soy sauce for serving

Instructions:

1. **Coat the tuna steaks:**
   Season the tuna steaks with salt and pepper. Press sesame seeds onto both sides of the tuna.
2. **Heat the skillet:**
   Heat the sesame oil in a skillet over medium-high heat.
3. **Sear the tuna:**
   Add the tuna steaks to the skillet and sear for 1-2 minutes per side, until the sesame seeds are toasted and the tuna is rare to medium-rare inside.
4. **Serve:**
   Slice the tuna and serve with soy sauce and a side of rice or vegetables.

Clam Chowder

Ingredients:

- 2 dozen clams, scrubbed and opened
- 4 cups clam juice (or seafood stock)
- 2 cups potatoes, peeled and diced
- 1/2 cup diced celery
- 1/2 cup diced onion
- 2 cloves garlic, minced
- 1 cup heavy cream
- 1 tablespoon butter
- 1 teaspoon thyme
- Salt and pepper to taste
- Fresh parsley for garnish

Instructions:

1. **Cook the clams:**
   In a large pot, steam the clams in clam juice until they open. Remove the clams, discard any unopened shells, and set the clams aside.
2. **Prepare the base:**
   In the same pot, melt butter over medium heat. Add the onions, garlic, celery, and potatoes. Cook until the vegetables are tender, about 10 minutes.
3. **Add the broth and simmer:**
   Add the clam juice and thyme, and bring to a simmer. Cook for 10 minutes, or until the potatoes are soft.
4. **Finish the chowder:**
   Stir in the cream and chopped clams. Season with salt and pepper. Simmer for 5 more minutes.
5. **Serve:**
   Garnish with fresh parsley and serve with crusty bread.

Shrimp Scampi

Ingredients:

- 1 lb large shrimp, peeled and deveined
- 4 tablespoons butter
- 4 cloves garlic, minced
- 1/4 cup dry white wine
- 1/4 cup chicken broth
- 2 tablespoons lemon juice
- 1/2 teaspoon red pepper flakes (optional)
- 1/2 cup fresh parsley, chopped
- Salt and pepper to taste
- 8 oz pasta (linguine or spaghetti)

Instructions:

1. **Cook the pasta:**
   Cook pasta according to package instructions. Drain and set aside.
2. **Cook the shrimp:**
   In a large skillet, melt butter over medium heat. Add garlic and cook for 1 minute until fragrant. Add shrimp and cook until pink and opaque, about 3-4 minutes.
3. **Make the sauce:**
   Add the white wine, chicken broth, lemon juice, and red pepper flakes (if using). Bring to a simmer and cook for 2-3 minutes.
4. **Combine with pasta:**
   Add the cooked pasta to the skillet and toss to combine. Season with salt and pepper.
5. **Serve:**
   Garnish with fresh parsley and serve hot.

Paella

Ingredients:

- 1 lb shrimp, peeled and deveined
- 1 lb chicken thighs, bone-in and skinless, cut into pieces
- 1/2 lb chorizo, sliced
- 1 bell pepper, chopped
- 1 onion, chopped
- 2 cloves garlic, minced
- 2 cups Arborio rice
- 4 cups chicken stock
- 1/4 teaspoon saffron threads
- 1 teaspoon paprika
- 1/2 teaspoon turmeric
- Salt and pepper to taste
- Lemon wedges for serving

Instructions:

1. **Cook the proteins:**
   In a large pan, cook the chicken pieces and chorizo over medium-high heat until browned. Remove and set aside.
2. **Cook the vegetables:**
   In the same pan, sauté the onion, bell pepper, and garlic until soft, about 5 minutes.
3. **Make the rice base:**
   Add the rice to the pan and cook for 2 minutes, stirring constantly. Add saffron, paprika, turmeric, and chicken stock. Bring to a boil, then reduce heat and simmer for 15 minutes.
4. **Add the seafood:**
   Add the shrimp and cooked chicken and chorizo back to the pan. Cook for an additional 5-7 minutes until the seafood is cooked through and the rice is tender.
5. **Serve:**
   Serve with lemon wedges.

Baked Salmon with Dill

Ingredients:

- 4 salmon fillets
- 2 tablespoons olive oil
- 1 tablespoon lemon juice
- 1 tablespoon Dijon mustard
- 1 teaspoon dried dill
- Salt and pepper to taste
- Fresh dill for garnish

Instructions:

1. **Prepare the salmon:**
   Preheat the oven to 375°F (190°C). Place the salmon fillets on a baking sheet lined with parchment paper.
2. **Season the salmon:**
   In a small bowl, whisk together olive oil, lemon juice, mustard, dill, salt, and pepper. Drizzle over the salmon fillets.
3. **Bake the salmon:**
   Bake for 15-20 minutes, or until the salmon is cooked through and flakes easily with a fork.
4. **Serve:**
   Garnish with fresh dill and serve with vegetables or rice.

Fish Tacos

Ingredients:

- 1 lb white fish fillets (such as tilapia or cod)
- 8 small corn tortillas
- 1/2 cup cabbage, shredded
- 1/4 cup cilantro, chopped
- 1/4 cup sour cream
- 2 tablespoons lime juice
- 1 teaspoon chili powder
- Salt and pepper to taste
- Hot sauce for serving (optional)

Instructions:

1. **Cook the fish:**
   Season the fish fillets with chili powder, salt, and pepper. Cook in a skillet over medium heat for 3-4 minutes per side, until the fish is cooked through.
2. **Prepare the toppings:**
   In a small bowl, mix sour cream with lime juice. Toss the cabbage with chopped cilantro.
3. **Assemble the tacos:**
   Warm the tortillas and place a piece of fish on each. Top with cabbage, cilantro, sour cream, and a drizzle of hot sauce.
4. **Serve:**
   Serve with extra lime wedges.

Lobster Bisque

Ingredients:

- 2 lobster tails, cooked and chopped
- 2 tablespoons butter
- 1/4 cup onion, finely chopped
- 2 cloves garlic, minced
- 1/4 cup tomato paste
- 2 cups chicken stock
- 1 cup heavy cream
- 1/2 cup brandy or sherry
- 1 teaspoon paprika
- Salt and pepper to taste
- Fresh parsley for garnish

Instructions:

1. **Prepare the bisque base:**
   In a pot, melt butter over medium heat. Add onion and garlic, cooking until softened. Stir in tomato paste and cook for another minute.
2. **Add liquids:**
   Slowly pour in the chicken stock and brandy, scraping up any bits stuck to the bottom of the pot. Bring to a simmer and cook for 10 minutes.
3. **Finish the bisque:**
   Add the lobster meat and heavy cream to the pot. Simmer for 5-7 minutes. Season with paprika, salt, and pepper.
4. **Serve:**
   Garnish with fresh parsley and serve hot.

Oysters Rockefeller

Ingredients:

- 12 fresh oysters, shucked
- 2 tablespoons butter
- 1/2 cup spinach, chopped
- 1/4 cup breadcrumbs
- 2 tablespoons Parmesan cheese
- 2 tablespoons Pernod or anise-flavored liqueur
- 1 teaspoon lemon juice
- 1 clove garlic, minced
- Salt and pepper to taste
- 1/4 cup fresh parsley, chopped

Instructions:

1. **Prepare the spinach mixture:**
   In a skillet, melt butter over medium heat. Add garlic and cook until fragrant. Add spinach and cook until wilted. Stir in breadcrumbs, Parmesan cheese, Pernod, lemon juice, salt, and pepper. Cook for 2-3 minutes.
2. **Assemble the oysters:**
   Preheat the oven broiler. Place the oysters on a baking sheet, spoon the spinach mixture onto each oyster.
3. **Broil the oysters:**
   Broil the oysters for 5-7 minutes, or until the topping is golden and bubbly.
4. **Serve:**
   Garnish with fresh parsley and serve hot.

Tuna Tartare

Ingredients:

- 1 lb sushi-grade tuna, diced
- 1/4 cup soy sauce
- 1 tablespoon sesame oil
- 1 tablespoon lime juice
- 1 teaspoon ginger, grated
- 1 small avocado, diced
- 1 tablespoon scallions, chopped
- 1 tablespoon sesame seeds
- 1 teaspoon chili flakes (optional)

Instructions:

1. **Prepare the tuna:**
   Dice the tuna into small cubes and place in a mixing bowl.
2. **Make the dressing:**
   In a small bowl, whisk together soy sauce, sesame oil, lime juice, ginger, and chili flakes (if using).
3. **Assemble the tartare:**
   Pour the dressing over the tuna and toss to coat. Add the diced avocado, scallions, and sesame seeds, and gently mix.
4. **Serve:**
   Spoon the tartare into serving dishes and garnish with extra sesame seeds and chili flakes. Serve with crackers or toasted bread.

Mussels in White Wine Sauce

Ingredients:

- 2 lbs mussels, cleaned and debearded
- 1 tablespoon butter
- 2 cloves garlic, minced
- 1/2 cup dry white wine
- 1/4 cup heavy cream
- 1/4 cup parsley, chopped
- Salt and pepper to taste
- Lemon wedges for serving

Instructions:

1. **Sauté the garlic:**
   In a large pot, melt butter over medium heat. Add garlic and cook until fragrant, about 1 minute.
2. **Cook the mussels:**
   Add the mussels to the pot and pour in the white wine. Cover and cook for 5-7 minutes, or until the mussels open.
3. **Make the sauce:**
   Remove the mussels and add heavy cream to the pot, stirring to combine. Season with salt and pepper.
4. **Serve:**
   Return the mussels to the pot and toss to coat. Garnish with fresh parsley and serve with lemon wedges.

Crab Cakes

Ingredients:

- 1 lb crab meat, drained and picked through for shells
- 1/2 cup breadcrumbs
- 2 tablespoons mayonnaise
- 1 tablespoon Dijon mustard
- 1 tablespoon Worcestershire sauce
- 1 egg, beaten
- 1 tablespoon parsley, chopped
- 1/2 teaspoon paprika
- Salt and pepper to taste
- 2 tablespoons butter, for frying

Instructions:

1. **Make the mixture:**
   In a bowl, combine crab meat, breadcrumbs, mayonnaise, Dijon mustard, Worcestershire sauce, egg, parsley, paprika, salt, and pepper. Mix gently.
2. **Form the cakes:**
   Shape the mixture into small patties, about 2-3 inches in diameter.
3. **Cook the crab cakes:**
   In a skillet, heat butter over medium heat. Add the crab cakes and cook for 3-4 minutes per side, until golden brown.
4. **Serve:**
   Serve the crab cakes with a squeeze of lemon and a side of tartar sauce.

Fish and Chips

Ingredients:

- 4 white fish fillets (such as cod or haddock)
- 1 cup all-purpose flour
- 1 teaspoon baking powder
- 1 teaspoon salt
- 1 cup sparkling water
- 1/2 teaspoon paprika
- 1/2 cup potato flour or cornstarch
- Vegetable oil, for frying
- Salt for seasoning
- 4 large potatoes, peeled and cut into fries

Instructions:

1. **Prepare the fries:**
   Heat oil in a large pot to 350°F (175°C). Fry the potato fries in batches for 3-4 minutes until golden. Drain and season with salt.
2. **Make the batter:**
   In a bowl, whisk together flour, baking powder, salt, paprika, and sparkling water to make a smooth batter.
3. **Fry the fish:**
   Dip the fish fillets into the batter, coating them evenly. Fry in hot oil for 4-5 minutes, until crispy and golden. Remove and drain on paper towels.
4. **Serve:**
   Serve the fish and chips with tartar sauce, lemon wedges, and vinegar.

Shrimp Cocktail

Ingredients:

- 1 lb large shrimp, peeled and deveined
- 1 tablespoon Old Bay seasoning
- 1 lemon, quartered
- 1 cup cocktail sauce

Instructions:

1. **Cook the shrimp:**
   Bring a pot of water to a boil, adding Old Bay seasoning and lemon. Add the shrimp and cook for 2-3 minutes until pink and cooked through. Drain and cool.
2. **Serve:**
   Arrange the shrimp on a platter with cocktail sauce for dipping. Garnish with lemon wedges.

Crab Legs with Garlic Butter

Ingredients:

- 2 lbs king crab legs, thawed
- 1/4 cup butter
- 3 cloves garlic, minced
- 1 tablespoon lemon juice
- 1 tablespoon fresh parsley, chopped
- Salt and pepper to taste

Instructions:

1. **Cook the crab legs:**
   Bring a large pot of water to a boil. Add the crab legs and cook for 5-7 minutes. Drain and set aside.
2. **Make the garlic butter:**
   In a small saucepan, melt butter over medium heat. Add garlic and cook until fragrant, about 1 minute. Stir in lemon juice and parsley.
3. **Serve:**
   Pour the garlic butter over the crab legs and serve with extra lemon wedges.

Grilled Mahi Mahi

Ingredients:

- 2 mahi mahi fillets
- 2 tablespoons olive oil
- 1 teaspoon garlic powder
- 1 teaspoon paprika
- 1 tablespoon lime juice
- Salt and pepper to taste

Instructions:

1. **Season the fish:**
   Brush the mahi mahi fillets with olive oil. Season with garlic powder, paprika, salt, and pepper.
2. **Grill the fish:**
   Preheat the grill to medium-high heat. Grill the fish for 3-4 minutes per side until cooked through.
3. **Serve:**
   Drizzle with lime juice and serve with grilled vegetables or a salad.

Smoked Salmon

Ingredients:

- 1 lb fresh salmon fillet, skin on
- 1/4 cup brown sugar
- 1/4 cup sea salt
- 1 tablespoon black peppercorns, cracked
- 1 tablespoon dill, chopped

Instructions:

1. **Prepare the salmon:**
   Mix brown sugar, sea salt, peppercorns, and dill in a small bowl. Rub the mixture all over the salmon fillet. Cover and refrigerate for 2-4 hours.
2. **Smoke the salmon:**
   Preheat your smoker to 225°F (107°C). Place the salmon on the smoker rack and smoke for 1.5-2 hours, until the fish is firm and fully cooked.
3. **Serve:**
   Slice the smoked salmon and serve with crackers, bagels, or a salad.

Shrimp and Grits

Ingredients:

- 1 lb large shrimp, peeled and deveined
- 1 cup stone-ground grits
- 4 cups water or chicken broth
- 1/2 cup heavy cream
- 1 tablespoon butter
- 1/2 cup cheddar cheese, shredded
- 1 tablespoon olive oil
- 2 cloves garlic, minced
- 1/2 teaspoon smoked paprika
- 1/4 teaspoon cayenne pepper
- Salt and pepper to taste
- 2 tablespoons scallions, chopped
- Lemon wedges for garnish

Instructions:

1. **Cook the grits:**
   Bring the water or chicken broth to a boil. Stir in the grits and reduce the heat to low. Cover and cook for 20-25 minutes, stirring occasionally. Once cooked, stir in heavy cream, butter, and cheddar cheese. Season with salt and pepper.
2. **Cook the shrimp:**
   In a large skillet, heat olive oil over medium heat. Add garlic and cook for 1 minute. Add shrimp, paprika, cayenne, salt, and pepper. Cook for 2-3 minutes on each side until pink and cooked through.
3. **Serve:**
   Spoon the grits onto plates and top with shrimp. Garnish with chopped scallions and lemon wedges.

Seafood Risotto

Ingredients:

- 1 lb mixed seafood (shrimp, scallops, mussels, etc.)
- 1 1/2 cups Arborio rice
- 1/2 cup white wine
- 4 cups seafood stock (or chicken stock)
- 1 small onion, finely chopped
- 2 cloves garlic, minced
- 2 tablespoons butter
- 1/2 cup Parmesan cheese, grated
- Salt and pepper to taste
- Fresh parsley, chopped for garnish

Instructions:

1. **Cook the seafood:**
   In a large skillet, cook the mixed seafood in a bit of butter over medium heat until just cooked through, about 4-5 minutes. Remove and set aside.
2. **Make the risotto:**
   In a separate pot, heat the remaining butter over medium heat. Add the onion and garlic and cook until softened. Stir in the Arborio rice and cook for 1-2 minutes. Add the white wine and cook until absorbed. Gradually add the seafood stock, one ladle at a time, stirring constantly until absorbed before adding more stock.
3. **Combine seafood and risotto:**
   When the rice is tender and creamy (about 18-20 minutes), stir in the cooked seafood and Parmesan cheese. Season with salt and pepper.
4. **Serve:**
   Garnish with fresh parsley and serve immediately.

Lobster Roll

Ingredients:

- 2 lobster tails, cooked and chopped
- 1/4 cup mayonnaise
- 1 tablespoon Dijon mustard
- 1 teaspoon lemon juice
- 2 tablespoons fresh chives, chopped
- Salt and pepper to taste
- 2 brioche rolls, toasted
- Butter, for toasting the rolls

Instructions:

1. **Prepare the lobster:**
   Boil or steam the lobster tails until cooked (about 6-8 minutes). Remove the meat and chop it into bite-sized pieces.
2. **Make the dressing:**
   In a bowl, combine mayonnaise, Dijon mustard, lemon juice, chives, salt, and pepper.
3. **Assemble the lobster roll:**
   Mix the lobster meat with the dressing and gently toss to coat.
4. **Toast the rolls:**
   Butter the brioche rolls and toast them in a skillet until golden brown.
5. **Serve:**
   Spoon the lobster mixture into the toasted rolls and serve immediately.

Grilled Octopus

Ingredients:

- 2 octopus tentacles (about 1-1.5 lbs)
- 1/4 cup olive oil
- 2 cloves garlic, minced
- 1 teaspoon smoked paprika
- 1 teaspoon lemon zest
- 2 tablespoons lemon juice
- Salt and pepper to taste
- Fresh parsley for garnish

Instructions:

1. **Tenderize the octopus:**
   Boil the octopus in water with salt for 40-45 minutes until tender. Drain and let it cool.
2. **Prepare the marinade:**
   In a bowl, whisk together olive oil, garlic, smoked paprika, lemon zest, lemon juice, salt, and pepper.
3. **Grill the octopus:**
   Preheat the grill to medium-high heat. Brush the octopus tentacles with the marinade and grill for 3-4 minutes on each side until charred.
4. **Serve:**
   Garnish with fresh parsley and serve with lemon wedges.

Shrimp Alfredo

Ingredients:

- 1 lb shrimp, peeled and deveined
- 1 tablespoon olive oil
- 2 cloves garlic, minced
- 1 cup heavy cream
- 1/2 cup Parmesan cheese, grated
- 1 teaspoon garlic powder
- Salt and pepper to taste
- 8 oz fettuccine pasta, cooked
- Fresh parsley, chopped for garnish

Instructions:

1. **Cook the shrimp:**
   In a large skillet, heat olive oil over medium heat. Add garlic and cook for 1 minute. Add shrimp, salt, pepper, and garlic powder. Cook for 2-3 minutes per side until pink and cooked through. Remove shrimp and set aside.
2. **Make the Alfredo sauce:**
   In the same skillet, add heavy cream and bring to a simmer. Stir in Parmesan cheese and cook until the sauce thickens, about 4-5 minutes.
3. **Combine the pasta and shrimp:**
   Add the cooked fettuccine to the skillet and toss to coat with the sauce. Add the shrimp back into the pan and toss again.
4. **Serve:**
   Garnish with fresh parsley and serve immediately.

Clams Casino

Ingredients:

- 12 fresh clams, shucked
- 1/2 cup breadcrumbs
- 1/4 cup Parmesan cheese, grated
- 2 tablespoons butter, melted
- 2 cloves garlic, minced
- 2 tablespoons parsley, chopped
- 1/4 teaspoon paprika
- 1/4 cup white wine

Instructions:

1. **Prepare the clams:**
   Preheat the oven to 400°F (200°C). Place the shucked clams in a baking dish.
2. **Make the topping:**
   In a bowl, combine breadcrumbs, Parmesan cheese, melted butter, garlic, parsley, and paprika. Spoon the mixture onto each clam.
3. **Bake the clams:**
   Drizzle white wine over the clams and bake for 10-12 minutes until the topping is golden and crispy.
4. **Serve:**
   Serve hot with lemon wedges.

Salmon with Mango Salsa

Ingredients:

- 4 salmon fillets
- 1 tablespoon olive oil
- Salt and pepper to taste
- 1 mango, diced
- 1/4 red onion, finely chopped
- 1 tablespoon lime juice
- 1 tablespoon cilantro, chopped

Instructions:

1. **Prepare the salmon:**
   Preheat the grill or skillet over medium heat. Rub the salmon fillets with olive oil, salt, and pepper. Cook for 3-4 minutes per side until the fish is cooked through.
2. **Make the salsa:**
   In a bowl, combine mango, red onion, lime juice, and cilantro. Season with salt and pepper.
3. **Serve:**
   Spoon the mango salsa over the cooked salmon fillets and serve.

Ceviche

Ingredients:

- 1 lb shrimp or white fish, diced
- 1/2 red onion, finely chopped
- 2 tomatoes, diced
- 1/4 cup cilantro, chopped
- 1 jalapeño, finely chopped
- 1/2 cup lime juice
- Salt and pepper to taste

Instructions:

1. **Marinate the seafood:**
   In a bowl, combine seafood with lime juice. Let it marinate for 1-2 hours in the refrigerator until the seafood is "cooked" by the acidity of the lime juice.
2. **Prepare the vegetables:**
   Add onion, tomatoes, cilantro, and jalapeño to the bowl. Season with salt and pepper.
3. **Serve:**
   Serve chilled with tortilla chips or tostadas.

Scallops with Lemon Butter

Ingredients:

- 1 lb sea scallops, patted dry
- 2 tablespoons butter
- 1 tablespoon olive oil
- 2 cloves garlic, minced
- 1 tablespoon lemon juice
- Salt and pepper to taste
- Fresh parsley, chopped for garnish

Instructions:

1. **Cook the scallops:**
   In a large skillet, heat olive oil and butter over medium-high heat. Season the scallops with salt and pepper. Sear the scallops for 2-3 minutes per side until golden brown.
2. **Make the lemon butter sauce:**
   Remove the scallops from the skillet. Add garlic to the skillet and cook for 30 seconds. Stir in lemon juice and cook for another 1 minute.
3. **Serve:**
   Return the scallops to the skillet and toss them in the lemon butter sauce. Garnish with parsley and serve.

Crab Stuffed Mushrooms

Ingredients:

- 12 large mushrooms, stems removed
- 1/2 lb crab meat, drained
- 1/4 cup cream cheese, softened
- 1/4 cup breadcrumbs
- 1/4 cup Parmesan cheese, grated
- 1 tablespoon parsley, chopped
- 1 tablespoon lemon juice
- Salt and pepper to taste

Instructions:

1. **Prepare the filling:**
   Preheat the oven to 375°F (190°C). In a bowl, combine crab meat, cream cheese, breadcrumbs, Parmesan cheese, parsley, lemon juice, salt, and pepper.
2. **Stuff the mushrooms:**
   Spoon the crab mixture into each mushroom cap.
3. **Bake the mushrooms:**
   Arrange the stuffed mushrooms on a baking sheet and bake for 15-20 minutes until golden and bubbly.
4. **Serve:**
   Serve immediately as an appetizer.

Blackened Snapper

Ingredients:

- 4 snapper fillets
- 2 tablespoons paprika
- 1 teaspoon garlic powder
- 1 teaspoon onion powder
- 1 teaspoon dried thyme
- 1/2 teaspoon cayenne pepper
- 1/2 teaspoon salt
- 1/2 teaspoon black pepper
- 1 tablespoon olive oil
- 1 tablespoon butter
- Fresh lemon wedges for serving

Instructions:

1. **Make the blackened seasoning:**
   In a small bowl, mix together paprika, garlic powder, onion powder, thyme, cayenne, salt, and black pepper.
2. **Season the snapper:**
   Pat the snapper fillets dry with paper towels. Rub the seasoning mixture generously on both sides of each fillet.
3. **Cook the snapper:**
   In a skillet, heat olive oil and butter over medium-high heat. Once the oil is hot, add the fillets and cook for 3-4 minutes per side until crispy and cooked through.
4. **Serve:**
   Serve the blackened snapper with lemon wedges.

Tuna Poke Bowl

Ingredients:

- 1 lb fresh tuna, diced into 1-inch cubes
- 1/4 cup soy sauce
- 1 tablespoon sesame oil
- 1 tablespoon rice vinegar
- 1 teaspoon honey or brown sugar
- 1 tablespoon sesame seeds
- 1 avocado, sliced
- 1 cucumber, sliced into matchsticks
- 1/2 cup edamame beans
- 1/4 cup shredded carrots
- 2 cups cooked sushi rice
- Fresh cilantro for garnish

Instructions:

1. **Prepare the tuna:**
   In a bowl, combine soy sauce, sesame oil, rice vinegar, and honey. Add the diced tuna and let it marinate for 10-15 minutes.
2. **Assemble the bowl:**
   In serving bowls, layer the cooked sushi rice, marinated tuna, avocado, cucumber, edamame, and shredded carrots.
3. **Garnish and serve:**
   Top the poke bowls with sesame seeds and fresh cilantro. Serve immediately.

Baked Cod with Herb Crust

Ingredients:

- 4 cod fillets
- 1/2 cup panko breadcrumbs
- 2 tablespoons fresh parsley, chopped
- 2 tablespoons fresh thyme, chopped
- 1 tablespoon lemon zest
- 1/4 cup grated Parmesan cheese
- 1/4 cup melted butter
- Salt and pepper to taste

Instructions:

1. **Prepare the breadcrumb mixture:**
   Preheat the oven to 400°F (200°C). In a bowl, combine panko breadcrumbs, parsley, thyme, lemon zest, Parmesan cheese, melted butter, salt, and pepper.
2. **Crust the cod:**
   Place the cod fillets on a baking sheet lined with parchment paper. Spoon the breadcrumb mixture evenly over each fillet, pressing lightly to adhere.
3. **Bake the cod:**
   Bake the cod for 12-15 minutes, or until the fish flakes easily with a fork.
4. **Serve:**
   Serve immediately with lemon wedges.

Grilled Shrimp Skewers

Ingredients:

- 1 lb large shrimp, peeled and deveined
- 2 tablespoons olive oil
- 2 cloves garlic, minced
- 1 teaspoon smoked paprika
- 1 teaspoon lemon zest
- 1 tablespoon lemon juice
- Salt and pepper to taste
- Skewers (wooden or metal)

Instructions:

1. **Prepare the shrimp marinade:**
   In a bowl, mix olive oil, garlic, smoked paprika, lemon zest, lemon juice, salt, and pepper.
2. **Marinate the shrimp:**
   Add the shrimp to the bowl and toss to coat. Let it marinate in the refrigerator for at least 15 minutes.
3. **Grill the shrimp:**
   Preheat the grill to medium-high heat. Thread the shrimp onto the skewers and grill for 2-3 minutes per side, or until pink and cooked through.
4. **Serve:**
   Serve the shrimp skewers with additional lemon wedges.

Fish Stew

Ingredients:

- 1 lb white fish fillets (cod, tilapia, etc.), cut into chunks
- 1/2 lb shrimp, peeled and deveined
- 2 tablespoons olive oil
- 1 onion, chopped
- 2 cloves garlic, minced
- 1 can (14.5 oz) diced tomatoes
- 2 cups fish stock or chicken broth
- 1 teaspoon paprika
- 1/2 teaspoon thyme
- Salt and pepper to taste
- 1 tablespoon fresh parsley, chopped

Instructions:

1. **Cook the vegetables:**
   In a large pot, heat olive oil over medium heat. Add onion and garlic and cook for 3-4 minutes until softened.
2. **Add the liquids and seasonings:**
   Stir in diced tomatoes, fish stock, paprika, thyme, salt, and pepper. Bring to a simmer.
3. **Add the seafood:**
   Add the fish chunks and shrimp to the pot. Simmer for 10-12 minutes, or until the fish is cooked through and the shrimp is pink.
4. **Serve:**
   Garnish with fresh parsley and serve hot.

Lobster Mac and Cheese

Ingredients:

- 1 lb elbow macaroni, cooked
- 1 lb lobster tail, cooked and chopped
- 2 cups shredded cheddar cheese
- 1 cup shredded Gruyère cheese
- 2 tablespoons butter
- 2 tablespoons flour
- 2 cups milk
- 1 teaspoon Dijon mustard
- Salt and pepper to taste
- 1/2 cup breadcrumbs (optional, for topping)

Instructions:

1. **Make the cheese sauce:**
   In a saucepan, melt butter over medium heat. Stir in flour and cook for 1-2 minutes. Gradually add milk, whisking constantly until the sauce thickens. Stir in cheddar and Gruyère cheeses, Dijon mustard, salt, and pepper.
2. **Combine the pasta and lobster:**
   Add the cooked macaroni and lobster meat to the cheese sauce. Stir to combine.
3. **Bake (optional):**
   Preheat the oven to 375°F (190°C). Transfer the mac and cheese to a baking dish, top with breadcrumbs, and bake for 15-20 minutes, until the top is golden and bubbly.
4. **Serve:**
   Serve the lobster mac and cheese hot.

Shrimp Tempura

Ingredients:

- 1 lb large shrimp, peeled and deveined
- 1 cup all-purpose flour
- 1/4 cup cornstarch
- 1 teaspoon baking powder
- 1/2 teaspoon salt
- 1 egg, beaten
- 1 cup ice-cold water
- Vegetable oil for frying
- Soy sauce or tempura dipping sauce for serving

Instructions:

1. **Make the batter:**
   In a bowl, whisk together flour, cornstarch, baking powder, and salt. Add the egg and ice-cold water, stirring until just combined (don't overmix).
2. **Fry the shrimp:**
   Heat oil in a deep pot or skillet to 375°F (190°C). Dip the shrimp in the batter and fry for 2-3 minutes, or until golden and crispy. Remove with a slotted spoon and drain on paper towels.
3. **Serve:**
   Serve the shrimp tempura with soy sauce or tempura dipping sauce.

Scallops and Asparagus

Ingredients:

- 12 large scallops
- 1 bunch asparagus, trimmed
- 2 tablespoons olive oil
- 1 tablespoon butter
- Salt and pepper to taste
- 1 tablespoon lemon juice
- 1 tablespoon fresh parsley, chopped

Instructions:

1. **Cook the asparagus:**
   In a skillet, heat olive oil over medium heat. Add the asparagus and sauté for 4-5 minutes until tender. Season with salt and pepper and set aside.
2. **Cook the scallops:**
   In the same skillet, melt butter over medium-high heat. Season the scallops with salt and pepper and sear for 2-3 minutes per side, until golden brown.
3. **Serve:**
   Plate the scallops with the asparagus and drizzle with lemon juice. Garnish with fresh parsley.

Mussels Marinara

Ingredients:

- 2 lbs fresh mussels, cleaned and debearded
- 2 tablespoons olive oil
- 4 cloves garlic, minced
- 1 can (14.5 oz) crushed tomatoes
- 1/4 cup white wine
- 1 teaspoon dried oregano
- Salt and pepper to taste
- Fresh basil for garnish

Instructions:

1. **Cook the garlic:**
   In a large pot, heat olive oil over medium heat. Add garlic and cook for 1 minute.
2. **Make the marinara sauce:**
   Stir in crushed tomatoes, white wine, oregano, salt, and pepper. Bring to a simmer and cook for 5-7 minutes.
3. **Cook the mussels:**
   Add the mussels to the pot and cover. Cook for 5-7 minutes, or until the mussels have opened.
4. **Serve:**
   Discard any unopened mussels. Garnish with fresh basil and serve with crusty bread.

Crab Louie Salad

Ingredients:

- 1 lb cooked crab meat (preferably lump)
- 4 cups mixed greens (lettuce, arugula, etc.)
- 1/2 cup cherry tomatoes, halved
- 1/4 cup cucumber, thinly sliced
- 2 boiled eggs, sliced
- 1/4 cup red onion, thinly sliced
- 1 avocado, sliced
- 1/4 cup sliced radishes
- 1/4 cup olives (optional)

Louie Dressing:

- 1/4 cup mayonnaise
- 2 tablespoons ketchup
- 1 tablespoon lemon juice
- 1 teaspoon Dijon mustard
- 1/2 teaspoon Worcestershire sauce
- 1/2 teaspoon hot sauce (optional)
- Salt and pepper to taste

Instructions:

1. **Make the dressing:**
   In a small bowl, whisk together all of the dressing ingredients until smooth. Adjust salt and pepper to taste.
2. **Prepare the salad:**
   On a large plate or serving platter, arrange the mixed greens. Top with cherry tomatoes, cucumber, boiled eggs, red onion, avocado, radishes, and olives if using.
3. **Add the crab:**
   Gently place the crab meat in the center or arrange it across the salad.
4. **Serve:**
   Drizzle with Louie dressing just before serving or serve the dressing on the side.

Lobster Tail with Garlic Butter

Ingredients:

- 4 lobster tails
- 1/2 cup butter, melted
- 3 cloves garlic, minced
- 1 tablespoon lemon juice
- 1 teaspoon paprika
- Salt and pepper to taste
- Fresh parsley, chopped (for garnish)

Instructions:

1. **Prepare the lobster tails:**
   Preheat the grill to medium-high heat. Using kitchen shears, cut the lobster tails down the center of the top shell, exposing the meat.
2. **Prepare the garlic butter:**
   In a small bowl, mix melted butter, garlic, lemon juice, paprika, salt, and pepper.
3. **Grill the lobster tails:**
   Brush the lobster meat with the garlic butter mixture. Place the lobster tails on the grill, shell-side down. Grill for 6-8 minutes until the meat is opaque and cooked through, brushing with more butter halfway through.
4. **Serve:**
   Garnish with fresh parsley and additional lemon wedges.

Fried Catfish

Ingredients:

- 4 catfish fillets
- 1 cup buttermilk
- 1 cup cornmeal
- 1/2 cup all-purpose flour
- 1 teaspoon garlic powder
- 1 teaspoon paprika
- Salt and pepper to taste
- Vegetable oil for frying

Instructions:

1. **Prepare the catfish:**
   Soak the catfish fillets in buttermilk for 20-30 minutes.
2. **Prepare the coating:**
   In a shallow dish, combine cornmeal, flour, garlic powder, paprika, salt, and pepper.
3. **Fry the catfish:**
   Heat oil in a deep fryer or skillet to 375°F (190°C). Dredge each fillet in the cornmeal mixture, ensuring an even coat. Fry for 4-5 minutes per side until golden and crispy.
4. **Serve:**
   Serve immediately with lemon wedges and tartar sauce.

Crab and Corn Chowder

Ingredients:

- 1 lb crab meat (preferably lump)
- 4 cups chicken or vegetable broth
- 1 1/2 cups whole milk
- 1 cup heavy cream
- 2 cups frozen or fresh corn kernels
- 1 onion, chopped
- 2 celery stalks, chopped
- 2 cloves garlic, minced
- 2 medium potatoes, peeled and diced
- 2 tablespoons butter
- Salt and pepper to taste
- Fresh parsley for garnish

Instructions:

1. **Cook the vegetables:**
   In a large pot, melt butter over medium heat. Add onion, celery, and garlic. Sauté until softened, about 5 minutes.
2. **Make the chowder base:**
   Add the potatoes, broth, and corn to the pot. Bring to a boil, then reduce to a simmer for 15-20 minutes until the potatoes are tender.
3. **Add the cream and crab:**
   Stir in the milk, heavy cream, and crab meat. Simmer for another 5-7 minutes, until heated through. Season with salt and pepper.
4. **Serve:**
   Garnish with fresh parsley and serve hot.

Mahi Mahi with Pineapple Salsa

Ingredients:

- 4 mahi mahi fillets
- 1 tablespoon olive oil
- 1 teaspoon paprika
- Salt and pepper to taste
- 1 cup fresh pineapple, diced
- 1/4 cup red bell pepper, diced
- 1/4 cup red onion, finely chopped
- 1 tablespoon cilantro, chopped
- 1 tablespoon lime juice

Instructions:

1. **Prepare the salsa:**
   In a bowl, combine pineapple, red bell pepper, red onion, cilantro, and lime juice. Mix well and set aside.
2. **Prepare the fish:**
   Preheat the grill or a skillet over medium-high heat. Brush the mahi mahi fillets with olive oil and season with paprika, salt, and pepper.
3. **Grill the mahi mahi:**
   Grill the fillets for 3-4 minutes per side, or until the fish is cooked through and flakes easily.
4. **Serve:**
   Top each mahi mahi fillet with the fresh pineapple salsa and serve immediately.

Shrimp and Lobster Ravioli

Ingredients:

- 1 package (12 oz) shrimp and lobster ravioli
- 2 tablespoons butter
- 1/4 cup olive oil
- 2 cloves garlic, minced
- 1/2 cup heavy cream
- 1/4 cup grated Parmesan cheese
- Fresh parsley, chopped for garnish

Instructions:

1. **Cook the ravioli:**
   Cook the ravioli according to package instructions, typically 4-5 minutes in boiling water.
2. **Make the sauce:**
   While the ravioli cooks, heat butter and olive oil in a skillet over medium heat. Add the garlic and cook for 1-2 minutes. Stir in heavy cream and Parmesan cheese, simmer for 3-4 minutes.
3. **Toss the ravioli:**
   Drain the ravioli and add it to the skillet with the sauce. Gently toss to coat the ravioli in the sauce.
4. **Serve:**
   Garnish with fresh parsley and serve hot.

Smoked Fish Dip

Ingredients:

- 8 oz smoked white fish (such as trout or haddock), flaked
- 8 oz cream cheese, softened
- 1/4 cup sour cream
- 2 tablespoons mayonnaise
- 2 tablespoons lemon juice
- 1 tablespoon fresh dill, chopped
- 1 teaspoon Worcestershire sauce
- Salt and pepper to taste

Instructions:

1. **Make the dip:**
   In a bowl, combine the smoked fish, cream cheese, sour cream, mayonnaise, lemon juice, dill, Worcestershire sauce, salt, and pepper. Mix well until smooth.
2. **Chill:**
   Refrigerate the dip for at least 30 minutes to let the flavors meld.
3. **Serve:**
   Serve the smoked fish dip with crackers, toasted baguette slices, or fresh vegetables.

Fish Casserole

Ingredients:

- 1 lb white fish fillets (such as cod or haddock)
- 1 cup cream of mushroom soup
- 1/2 cup sour cream
- 1/2 cup grated cheese (cheddar or mozzarella)
- 1/4 cup breadcrumbs
- 1 tablespoon butter
- 1 tablespoon lemon juice
- 1 teaspoon garlic powder
- Salt and pepper to taste
- Fresh parsley for garnish

Instructions:

1. **Prepare the fish:**
   Preheat the oven to 350°F (175°C). Place the fish fillets in a greased casserole dish. Season with salt, pepper, and lemon juice.
2. **Make the sauce:**
   In a separate bowl, combine the cream of mushroom soup, sour cream, garlic powder, and grated cheese. Mix well and pour over the fish fillets.
3. **Top the casserole:**
   Sprinkle the breadcrumbs on top of the fish and sauce. Dot with butter.
4. **Bake:**
   Bake for 25-30 minutes, until the fish is cooked through and the top is golden and bubbly.
5. **Serve:**
   Garnish with fresh parsley and serve hot.

Clam Bake

Ingredients:

- 2 dozen clams (littleneck or steamers)
- 4 lobster tails
- 1 lb shrimp, peeled and deveined
- 4 ears of corn, husked and halved
- 4 small potatoes, halved
- 1/4 cup melted butter
- 2 cloves garlic, minced
- 1 lemon, sliced
- Fresh herbs (parsley, thyme, or rosemary)
- Salt and pepper to taste

Instructions:

1. **Prepare the clams and lobster:**
   Scrub the clams to remove any sand. If using lobster tails, cut them down the center of the shell to expose the meat.
2. **Assemble the bake:**
   In a large pot or a seafood steam basket, layer the clams, lobster tails, shrimp, corn, and potatoes. Add lemon slices and herbs for flavor. Sprinkle with salt and pepper.
3. **Steam the seafood:**
   Cover and steam over medium heat for 15-20 minutes, or until the clams have opened, the lobster is cooked through, and the potatoes are tender.
4. **Serve:**
   Drizzle with melted butter and garlic. Serve immediately with extra lemon wedges and fresh herbs.

Grilled Tuna Steaks

Ingredients:

- 4 tuna steaks
- 2 tablespoons olive oil
- 2 tablespoons soy sauce
- 1 tablespoon lemon juice
- 1 teaspoon Dijon mustard
- Salt and pepper to taste

Instructions:

1. **Marinate the tuna:**
   In a small bowl, whisk together olive oil, soy sauce, lemon juice, Dijon mustard, salt, and pepper. Place the tuna steaks in a shallow dish and pour the marinade over them. Let it marinate for at least 30 minutes.
2. **Grill the tuna:**
   Preheat the grill to medium-high heat. Grill the tuna steaks for 3-4 minutes per side for medium-rare, or longer if you prefer your tuna more cooked.
3. **Serve:**
   Serve the grilled tuna steaks with a side of grilled vegetables or a fresh salad.

Salmon Croquettes

Ingredients:

- 1 can (14.75 oz) salmon, drained and flaked
- 1/4 cup breadcrumbs
- 2 tablespoons mayonnaise
- 1 tablespoon Dijon mustard
- 1 egg, beaten
- 1 tablespoon fresh dill, chopped
- 1 tablespoon lemon juice
- 1/4 teaspoon garlic powder
- Salt and pepper to taste
- 2 tablespoons olive oil (for frying)

Instructions:

1. **Make the mixture:**
   In a bowl, combine the flaked salmon, breadcrumbs, mayonnaise, mustard, egg, dill, lemon juice, garlic powder, salt, and pepper. Mix until well combined.
2. **Form the croquettes:**
   Shape the mixture into small patties (about 2-3 inches in diameter).
3. **Fry the croquettes:**
   Heat the olive oil in a large skillet over medium heat. Fry the salmon croquettes for 3-4 minutes per side, until golden brown and crispy.
4. **Serve:**
   Serve with a squeeze of lemon or a dipping sauce like tartar sauce.

Fish En Papillote

Ingredients:

- 4 white fish fillets (such as cod, haddock, or sole)
- 1 lemon, sliced
- 1 small zucchini, thinly sliced
- 1 small red bell pepper, thinly sliced
- 2 cloves garlic, minced
- 1 tablespoon olive oil
- Fresh herbs (such as thyme, rosemary, or dill)
- Salt and pepper to taste
- Parchment paper

Instructions:

1. **Prepare the fish packets:**
   Preheat the oven to 400°F (200°C). Cut 4 large pieces of parchment paper. Place a fish fillet in the center of each piece of parchment.
2. **Add the vegetables and seasonings:**
   Top each fillet with lemon slices, zucchini, bell pepper, garlic, and fresh herbs. Drizzle with olive oil and season with salt and pepper.
3. **Seal the packets:**
   Fold the parchment paper over the fish and vegetables, crimping the edges to seal the packets.
4. **Bake:**
   Place the packets on a baking sheet and bake for 12-15 minutes, until the fish is cooked through.
5. **Serve:**
   Carefully open the packets and serve the fish with the vegetables.

Shrimp and Spinach Salad

Ingredients:

- 1 lb shrimp, peeled and deveined
- 4 cups fresh spinach
- 1/2 red onion, thinly sliced
- 1/4 cup feta cheese, crumbled
- 1/4 cup toasted pine nuts
- 1/4 cup olive oil
- 2 tablespoons balsamic vinegar
- 1 teaspoon Dijon mustard
- 1 garlic clove, minced
- Salt and pepper to taste

Instructions:

1. **Cook the shrimp:**
   Heat 1 tablespoon olive oil in a skillet over medium heat. Add the shrimp and cook for 2-3 minutes per side until pink and cooked through. Remove from the skillet and set aside.
2. **Make the dressing:**
   In a small bowl, whisk together the remaining olive oil, balsamic vinegar, Dijon mustard, garlic, salt, and pepper.
3. **Assemble the salad:**
   In a large bowl, toss the spinach, red onion, feta cheese, and pine nuts. Add the cooked shrimp and drizzle with the dressing.
4. **Serve:**
   Toss everything together and serve immediately.

www.ingramcontent.com/pod-product-compliance
Lightning Source LLC
LaVergne TN
LVHW081341060526
838201LV00055B/2775